NEW LET'S L

ENGLISH

3

CW01664403

Longman

DON DALLAS LINDA PELHAM

Contents

1 My friend

A Listen and look. Who can you see? Talk about the children.

I can see Sally. She's clever.

1 
lazy

2 
hard-working

3 

clever

4 
helpful

5 
naughty

6 
happy

7 
kind

8 
funny

B Listen and read. Where do the children live?

1

What do the children like doing? Ask and answer.

2

C Fun Reading

1 Tim cannot find his mother.

2

3

The police officer calls for help.

4

5 Suddenly, Tim sees a little dog.

6

D **Beeno is talking about his friends. Read and complete.**

This is my friend, Peter.
He's eight.
He lives in Sunset Road.
He goes to school by bus.
He likes sleeping.
I think he's lazy.

nine / Hill Road / train

This is my friend, Sally.

She's ~~nine~~ nine.

She lives in ~~Hill road~~ Hill road.

She goes to school by a train.

She likes reading books.

I think she's ~~Adventures~~ Smart.

Name: Charlie

Age: eight

Lives in: Wood Street

Goes to school by school bus

Likes: playing tricks

E Read.

This is Jack.

Jack likes playing tricks.

He does not like doing his homework.

This is John.

John likes reading.

He likes helping at home too.

What do you think about Jack and John? Write.

lazy	naughty	clever	dirty	kind
helpful	hard-working	happy	funny	polite

1 I think Jack is ~~lazy~~ lazy and ~~naughty~~ naughty but he is clever.

2 I think John is polite, hard working and happy.

2 My toys

A Listen and look. What can you see in the room?

There's a puzzle. It's on the shelf.

1 

a puzzle

2 

a plane

3 

a toy truck

4 

a spaceship

5 

a computer

6 

a robot

7 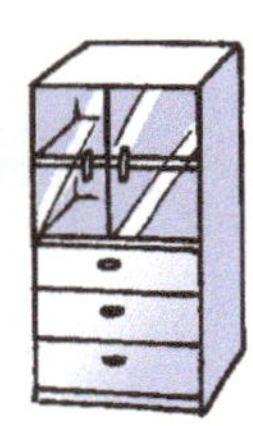

a cupboard

8 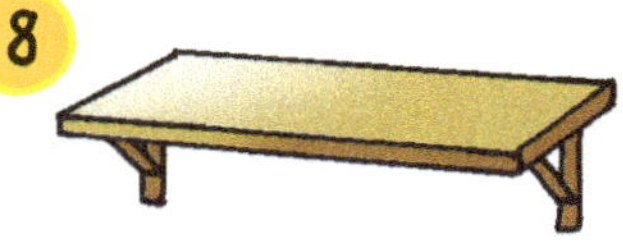

a shelf

B Listen and read. Talk about the toys.

1

2

C Fun Reading

1

2 The boys buy the blue cars.

3

4 The children play with their new cars. They do not see Charlie. He is behind a bush.

5

Charlie is naughty.
He is playing a trick on them.

6

D Look and read. Talk about the children's drawings.

1

I've got a bike.
This is my bike.
I keep it in my bedroom.

Peter's got a bike.
That's his bike.
He keeps it in his bedroom.

2

I've got six balls.
These are my balls.
I keep them in my cupboard.

Sally's got six balls.
Those are her balls.
She keeps them in her cupboard.

3

E Read and match. Write the numbers in the boxes.

1 I've got one bike.
This is my bike.
I keep it in my bedroom behind the door.

2 I've got two puzzles.
These are my puzzles.
I keep them in my toy box near the bed.

3 I've got three robots.
These are my robots.
I keep them on the shelf near the door.

4 I've got one rabbit.
This is my rabbit.
I keep it on my bed.

5 I've got one computer.
This is my computer.
I keep it on the desk in my bedroom.

3 Tasting things

A Listen and look. Talk about the tastes of the food.

1 
sugar

2 
salt

3 

honey

4 

vinegar

5 
chilli peppers

6 
pepper

B Listen and read. Talk about the food.

Finish Beeno's notes. Which food is ...? Write the names here.

sweet	Honey
salty	crisps
sour	Vinigar . lemon
hot	Peppa

C Fun Reading

1 Tom and Beeno are in a restaurant.

2 Beeno likes tasting new food.

3

4

5 The waiter takes their order.

6

D Play this game.

E Read and match. Write the letters in the boxes.

1 C

2 E

3 A

4 B

5 D

A Beeno: Can I have something sweet, please?
Tom: Here you are. This is honey.

B Beeno: Is there anything hot?
Tom: Yes, these are chilli peppers. Try some.

C Beeno: What are these, Tom?
Tom: They're lemons.

D Beeno: Oh dear! It's too hot. Give me some water. Quick!

E Beeno: Mmm. I like them.
Tom: Yes, I like lemons too.

Write.

Beeno likes ______________________________ .

Beeno does not like ______________________________ .

Units 1–3

Revision 1

A Look, ask and answer.

Now ask your friend where he or she lives.

B Match and write.

1 This is my computer [B]

2 That is my spaceship. [D]

3 That is his truck. [A]

4 This is her robot. [E]

5 These are my teddy bears. [F]

6 Those are my rabbits. [C]

A

B

C

D

E

F

C Ask and answer.

sour	sweet	salty	hot

D What do you and your friend like doing? Fill in the table.

	 helping at home	 reading	 playing computer games	 playing football	 drawing	 swimming
You	✓	✓	✓	✓	✓	✓
Your friend	✓	✓	don't know how to	✓	✓	✓

Now talk about you and your friend.

E Read: Jim and Betty.

Hello. My name is Jim. I live in Eastbourne. I am nine. I like reading and playing football. I have got very nice toys. My favourite toys are a spaceship and a kite. I keep them in the cupboard. I also like watching videos. After school I like playing computer games.

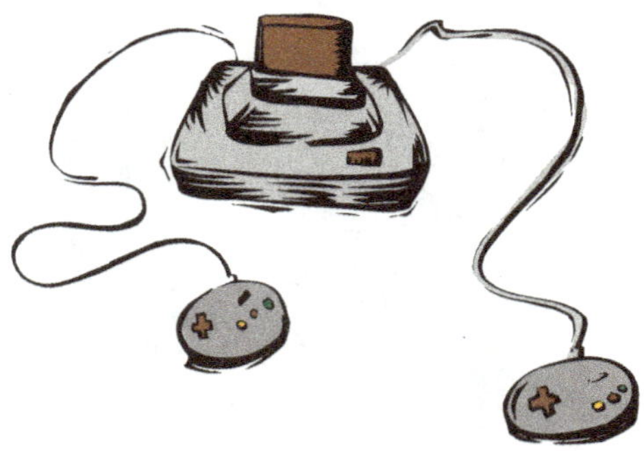

This is my sister, Betty. She is seven. Betty likes computer games and listening to music, too. She likes playing with her dolls. She has got two dolls. She calls them Milly and Lilly. She also has got two toy rabbits. She keeps the dolls and the rabbits on her bed.

4 Eating out

A Listen and look. What are they eating and drinking?

Mary is eating apple pie.
Tom's mother is drinking coffee.

1 
potatoes

2 
pasta

3 
roast chicken

4 
meat balls

5 
fruit salad

6 
apple pie

7 

tea

8 
coffee

B Listen and read. Bunny and Kitty are in a restaurant.

Now you are Kitty. Ask Bunny what he wants for lunch.

C Fun Reading

1 One day, Mrs Monkey, Mr Cat and Miss Rabbit meet Mr Tiger.

2

3

4

5

Choose the best title:

- [ ] The Hungry Animals
- [ ] The Tiger and his Friends
- [x] Dinner with Mr Tiger

D The family are in a restaurant. Talk about the menu.

SET DINNER

Soup of the day

Meat balls *or* Pasta *or* Roast Chicken

Ice cream *or* Fruit

Tea *or* Coffee

What do they order? Tell the teacher.

E Read.

Peter Sue

Set Lunch £10					
1	Fish	&	Rice or Chips	&	Fruit salad or Apple pie
2	Fish or Chicken	&	Rice or Vegetables	&	Tea or Orange juice
3	Chicken or Meat balls	&	Rice or Potatoes	&	Cake or Ice cream

Paul Ann

Peter: I want fish. I want chips but I don't want fruit salad. What do you want, Sue?

Sue: I want fish too. I want rice but I don't want tea.

Peter: What does Paul want?

Sue: He wants chicken. He wants vegetables but he doesn't want orange juice.

Peter: What does Ann want?

Sue: She wants chicken. She wants rice but she doesn't want cake.

Whose dishes are these? Write.

Sue	Paul	Anne	Peter

5 Buying things

A Listen and look. What is in the shops?

There's a fruit basket. It's in the fruit shop.
There are some boots. They're in the clothes shop.

1 

biscuits

2 
a fruit basket

3 
a pot plant

4 
an umbrella

5 
a raincoat

6 
boots

7 
jeans

8 
socks

B Listen and read. Talk about Charlie's shopping list.

Where do we buy chicken?

We buy chicken in a supermarket.

Where do we buy puzzles?

We buy puzzles in a toy shop.

The children are at the supermarket. Ask and answer questions about the food and drinks.

How much is the fish?

It's three pounds.

How much are the biscuits?

They're five pounds.

C Fun Reading

1

It is raining. Charlie and Cherry are going shopping with their mother.

2

Cherry is buying a new raincoat and a pair of boots.

3

Charlie is buying a new watch.

4

It is not raining now. Charlie and Cherry are sad. Then Charlie has a good idea.

5

It is wet in the fountain. Charlie and Cherry are happy now. Cherry is wearing her new raincoat and boots. Charlie is wearing his new watch.

Finish the sentences.

Charlie is clever. (clever / polite / hard-working)

He has a good idea. He plays under fountain.
(buys a watch / goes shopping with his mother / plays under the fountain)

D **The children are buying a birthday present for Betty. They have three pounds each. Ask and answer.**

E Read and match. Write the letters in the bubbles.

A Where do we buy them?	**B** Oh, yes!
C Yes, let's go now!	**D** Good idea, Mum. I like shopping. What things can we buy?

1 Betty, it's Aunt Helen's birthday on Saturday. Let's have a party for her.

2 Let's go shopping for the party now.

3 We can buy some chocolates, orange juice and biscuits, and a card for Aunt Helen.

A

4 We buy them in the supermarket and the book shop. Can we go now?

A

Answer the questions.

1 Whose birthday is it?

It is Aunt helen ____________.

2 When is her birthday?

It is on Saturda ____________.

3 Do Betty and her mother buy a birthday card?

yes ____________

6 School rules

A Listen and look. Talk about the children.

Look at Mary. She's running.
Look at Tom. He's playing football in the classroom.

1 
running

2 
walking

3 
talking

4 
keeping quiet

5 
eating

6 
playing

7 
sitting still

B Listen and read. Ken is a prefect.

1

2

Now you are Ken.

3

4

Match the pictures with the sentences. Write the numbers in the boxes.

- [1] You must walk in the corridor.
- [3] You mustn't play in the hall.
- [4] You mustn't eat in the classroom.
- [2] You must keep quiet in the library.

C Fun Reading

D Sally is visiting Beeno's school. Act Sally.

1

2

3

4

5

Now help the headmaster to write the rules for Beeno's school.

School rules

1 Do not play in the canteen.

2 Keep quiet in the library.

3 ______________________

4 ______________________

5 ______________________

E Read and match. Write the letters in the bubbles.

A Go back to your seats. Don't play in the classroom.

B You must work really hard. Be a good boy.

C Ready. Go.

D Can you see the sign, Tim and Joe? You must keep quiet.

E You must wear your school uniform.

F Stand still. Look here. One, two, three, OK.

1

2

3

4

What is the teacher saying in picture 2? Write.

G: ______________________________

Units 4–6

Revision 2

A Ask and answer.

Do you like meat balls?

Do you like pasta?

Yes, I do.

No, I don't.

meat balls

pasta

rice

roast chicken

fish

fruit salad

ice cream

potatoes

tea

orange juice

B Look and choose. Ask and answer.

flower shop	supermarket	bookshop
clothes shop	toy shop	shoe shop

Where do we buy shoes?

We buy shoes in a shoe shop.

C Talk about the food and drink.

D Talk about each picture. Use *must* or *mustn't*.

walk	run	keep quiet	talk	eat	play

E Read: At the Shopping Centre.

It's Saturday afternoon and Tim and Tina are shopping with their mother. They go to a big shopping centre. The shopping centre is a big building outside the town. It has got many different types of shops. It has also got restaurants, snack bars and a big cinema.

Tim and Tina's mother goes to the supermarket. She buys chicken, rice and some vegetables. Then she takes the children to a sports shop. She buys a pair of trainers for Tim in the sports shop. Then they go to a book shop. Here mother buys a story book for Tina. After that they are very hungry and they all go to a fast food restaurant. Finally, mother and the children go to the cinema. They see a funny film called 'My Uncle Joe'.

7 Sports

A Listen and look. What are the children doing?

They are playing tennis.
They are doing athletics.

B Listen and read. Beeno is learning about sports.
Ask and answer.

1

2

Talk about the other sports.

C Fun Reading

D Class survey. Find out how many children like the sports.

Which sports do you like?

Do you like skiing?

I like tennis and athletics.

No, I don't.

Sports		How many children?
	football	
	basketball	
	tennis	
	table tennis	
	athletics	
	skiing	

Now tell the class.

E Read.

1

2

3

4

5

6

Right (✓) or wrong (✗)?

1 ☐ Charlie and Betty are at school.

2 ☐ Charlie is drawing an orange.

3 ☐ Betty is drawing a tennis racket.

4 ☐ Charlie has got a new tennis racket.

5 ☐ Charlie likes basketball.

6 ☐ Betty does not like basketball.

7 ☐ Charlie plays tennis every day.

8 ☐ Betty plays basketball every Saturday.

8 On the beach

A Listen and look. Talk about the children.

He is windsurfing.
She is flying a kite.

B Listen and read. Mary and her friends are talking about activities on the beach.

Do you like snorkelling?

Yes, I do.

Does your brother like flying a kite?

Yes, he does.

Does your dad like windsurfing?

No, he doesn't.

Now you talk about your family.

Do you like roller skating?

Yes, I do.

Does your sister like cycling?

No, she doesn't.

C Fun Reading

1

2

3

4

D Emma and Ann are at the Beach Club.
Read about what they like and don't like doing.

Now put a tick (✓) or a cross (✗).

	swimming	snorkelling	windsurfing	flying a kite
Emma				
Ann				

Talk about Emma and Ann.

E Read and match. Write the letters in the boxes.

1 

2 

3 

4 

5 

A Ed runs after the kite but it flies too fast and too high. Ed can't catch his kite. He is very sad.

B Ed loves flying kites. For his birthday he gets a beautiful kite from his parents. Ed is very happy about his present.

C On his way home, Ed walks past a tree. He sees a string hanging from it. Ed pulls on the string.

D Ed goes to the park every day to fly his kite. It is his favourite toy.

E One day it is very windy. The kite flies very high. The wind is very strong and the kite flies away.

Tick the best picture to finish the story.

At the end of the string is a balloon. Ed takes it home.

At the end of the string is Ed's beautiful kite. It falls straight into his arms. Ed is happy again.

9 The 'helpful' boy

A Read and listen to the story.

1 Fred is on his way to school. He likes helping people.

2 Fred helps an old lady to cross the road.

3 Fred meets Mrs Johnson.

4 The bags are heavy. Fred cannot carry them.

5 Fred opens the door for a man.

6

7 The train is full.

8

9 Fred wants to help his teacher.

10

11 Fred is a good friend.

12 Fred is hungry. He wants some lunch but he's got no money.

B Read the story again. Then choose the correct answers.

Picture 3: Mrs Johnson is ______________________ .

a) reading b) shopping c) running

Picture 5: The man is ______________________ .

a) running b) walking c) shopping

Picture 8: The man is ______________________ .

a) happy b) kind c) rude

Picture 10: The teacher is ______________________ .

a) helpful b) unhappy c) afraid

C Read these words about Fred. Put a tick (✓) or a cross (✗).

Fred is:

kind	☐
lazy	☐
clever	☐
friendly	☐
funny	☐
helpful	☐
naughty	☐

What do you think of Fred? Tell your friend.

D What are the people saying? Look and match.

1

2

3

4

5

6

A Yes, please.

B I'm sorry. I can't hear you.

C Excuse me.

D No, thank you.

E You're welcome.

F I'm sorry. I don't know.

E Read and tick the correct responses.

1 Can I sit down here?

- [ ] Yes, of course.
- [ ] Good morning.

2 Excuse me. Where's the bus stop?

- [ ] Thank you.
- [ ] I'm sorry. I don't know.

3 Do you want ice cream?

- [ ] That's all right.
- [ ] Yes, please.

4 You're standing on my foot!

- [ ] Oh, I'm sorry.
- [ ] Here you are.

5 Thank you for carrying my bags.

- [ ] Goodbye, Mr Brown.
- [ ] You're welcome.

6 Good morning, Mr Smith. How are you?

- [ ] I'm fine, thank you.
- [ ] Excuse me.

Units 7–9

Revision 3

A What are the children doing? Ask and answer.

What are the children doing in picture 1?

They're playing tennis.

1

2

3

4

5

6

7

8

B Look at the pictures in Activity A. Which sports do you do in summer and which in winter? Talk to a friend.

Which sports do you do in summer?

Which sports do you do in winter?

I play badminton and I go swimming in summer.

I go skiing in winter.

Do you and your friend do the same sports in summer and in winter? Tell the class.

C Read and write the correct numbers next to the pictures.

1 
Ann

My sister likes doing athletics.

2 
Tim

My brother likes cycling.

3 
Sarah

My brother likes windsurfing.

4 
Emma

My sister likes roller skating.

5 
Jon

My brother likes snorkelling.

D Find out which sports your friend likes and doesn't like.

Which sports do you like?

I like football, basketball and tennis.

Do you like athletics?

No, I don't.

Now tell the class about your friend.

My friend Alex likes …

E Read: Popular Sports.

Football is the world's most popular sport. It is a team sport. A football team has got eleven players. A team wins by scoring goals. The players must kick the ball. They try to kick the ball into the other team's goal. Only the goal keeper can pick up the ball. The other ten players mustn't pick up the ball. The most famous football competition is the World Cup.

Tennis is another very popular sport. The players stand in an area called a court. They stand behind a net. They hit a tennis ball to each other with a racket. The ball must go over the net. It mustn't hit the net and it mustn't go out of the court. In some games there are only two players. This is called singles. In other games two players play two other players. This is called doubles. The most famous tennis competition is Wimbledon. Wimbledon is in London.

10 After school

A Listen and look. Talk about the subjects and activities the children like.

Peter

Sally

Betty

Tom

Charlie

Mary

What subject does Peter like? He likes English.
What does he like doing? He likes reading and writing.

1 
reading

2 
writing

3 

thinking

4 
running

5 
jumping

6 
painting

7 
singing

B Listen and read. Sally gets a letter from her pen friend Helen.

Dear Sally,

How are you? Do you enjoy school? I do.

What subjects do you like? I like English and I am good at reading. I read two story books every week. I also like painting and I am good at art but I do not like Music. I am not good at singing. What are you good at?

Please write soon.

Yours,
Helen

Now help Sally to finish her letter to Helen.

like	good at	do not like	not good at
French	writing	Art	painting
Maths	thinking		

Dear Helen,

Thank you for your letter. I enjoy school too. I like ________________ and

I am good at ____

____

____

____

____

Yours,

Sally

C Fun Reading

Act the story.

D Act the children.

Join a club after school

Sports Club

French Club

English Club

Art Club

Music Club

E Read and write the numbers. There is one picture too many.

a 

b 

c 

d 

1 This is John. He's very strong. He plays football. He likes running. He's good at sports.

2 This is Billy. He's very kind. He has lots of friends. He likes animals. He's good at drawing.

3 This is Paul. He's very clever. He's good at Maths and English. He likes thinking and writing.

11 Fun in the park

A **Listen and look. What can you see in the park?**

There are swings. They're in front of the slide.
There's a climbing frame. It's opposite the swimming pool.
There's a roller coaster. It's behind the climbing frame.

1 

a slide

2 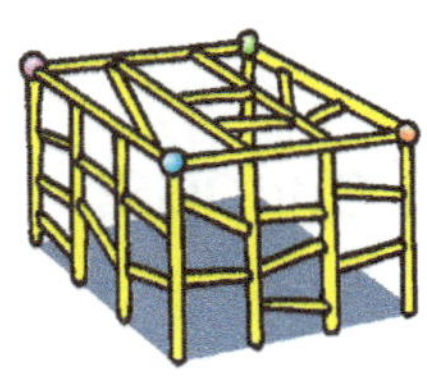

a climbing frame

3 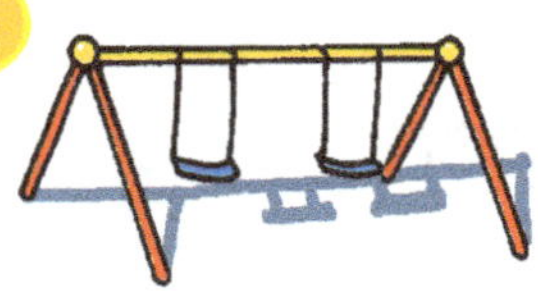

swings

4 

a cable car

5 

a roller coaster

6 

in front of

7 

behind

8 

opposite

B Listen and read. Tom and Beeno are in the park.

Tom: Where's the slide?
Beeno: Turn right here. It's behind the swings.
Tom: Where's the climbing frame?
Beeno: Turn left there. It's in front of the roller coaster.
Tom: Where's the cable car?
Beeno: Turn right there. It's opposite the slide.

You want to go to other places in the park. Ask and answer questions with your friends.

C Fun Reading

Choose the best title:

- ☐ The Rain Forest
- ☐ Charlie and the Monster
- ☐ A Ride on the Little Train

D Tom and Mary are asking the way to different places in the park. Ask and answer.

1

Mary:	What do you like doing in the park?
Tom:	I like riding on the roller coaster.
Mary:	Where's the roller coaster?
Tom:	I don't know. Let's ask that man.

2

Tom:	Excuse me. Where's the roller coaster, please?
Park keeper:	Turn right there. It's opposite the shops.
Tom:	Thank you.
Park keeper:	You're welcome.

E Read and match. Write the letters in the boxes.

1

☐

2

☐

3

☐

4

☐

5

☐

6

☐

A He is drawing on the picture.
B He likes drawing too.
C Charlie likes watching TV.
D Father sees the picture. He is angry.
E Look! Charlie is looking at his father's picture. What is he thinking?
F Charlie is under the desk. He is laughing.

Fill in the blanks.

Charlie is clever but ______________________ .

He likes playing ___________________________ .

12 Our birthdays

A **Listen and read. Ask and answer questions about the dates.**

MAY

MONDAY	TUESDAY	WEDNESDAY	THURSDAY	FRIDAY	SATURDAY	SUNDAY
1st first	2nd second	3rd Picnic third	4th fourth	5th fifth	6th sixth	7th seventh
8th eighth	9th ninth	10th tenth	11th Holiday eleventh	12th twelfth	13th thirteenth	14th fourteenth
15th TEST fifteenth	16th sixteenth	17th seventeenth	18th eighteenth	19th nineteenth	20th twentieth	21st twenty-first
22nd My Birthday twenty-second	23rd twenty-third	24th twenty-fourth	25th twenty-fifth	26th twenty-sixth	27th twenty-seventh	28th twenty-eighth
29th twenty-ninth	30th EXAM thirtieth	31st thirty-first				

B Listen and read. Ask and answer questions about the children's birthdays.

2005			
January	February	March	April
May	June	July	August
September	October	November	December

1

2

Ask about your friends' birthdays.

C Read about Billy.

This is Billy.
His birthday is on 29th February.
He has one birthday every four years.
Poor Billy!

Can you remember how many days there are in each month? Here is a rhyme to help you.

Thirty days have September,
April, June and November.
All the rest have thirty-one
Excepting February alone,
Which has but twenty-eight days clear
And twenty-nine in each leap year.

How many days are there in your birthday month? Finish the sentences.

My birthday is in ________________ . There are ________________ days in ________________ .

D The children are ordering birthday cakes. Ask and answer.

1

2

3

4

E Read and finish the dialogue.

A What does she like?	**B** Let's buy her a card too.
C Do you remember?	**D** It's today, the second of December.

1

May: When's Susie's birthday? ☐

Paul: Oh! ☐

2

May: Let's buy her a present. ☐

Paul: I think she likes flowers.

3

May: Let's buy her some flowers then.

Paul: OK. ☐

Units 10-12

Revision 4

A Talk about the children in the pictures.

What subject does Tom like?

What does Ted like doing?

He likes Maths.

He likes jumping.

1

Tom

2

Ted

3

Ann

4

Jim

5

Wendy

6

Ruth

What subjects do you like? Tell the class.

B Look at the pictures. Talk about Park A and Park B.

In Park A the slide is in front of the swings.

Yes, and the climbing frame is …

in front of opposite behind

A

B

C Talk about the children's birthdays.

1

Sally

2

Tim

3

Sue

4

Carol

5

John

D A survey. Choose six children from your class and find out when their birthdays are. Then put the information in the calendar.

January __________ __________	February __________ __________	March __________ __________	April __________ __________
May __________ __________	June __________ __________	July __________ __________	August __________ __________
September __________ __________	October __________ __________	November __________ __________	December __________ __________

When are the children's birthdays? Tell the class.

E Read: Super Park.

In the school holidays Jim and Joe visit Super Park with their dad. There are lots of interesting things in Super Park. There is a big roller coaster. It is very high and fast. Joe likes the roller coaster, but Jim doesn't like it. The roller coaster is opposite the snack bar.

There are swings in Super Park. The swings are next to the restaurant. Jim likes to go on the swings.

There is a big swimming pool. Jim, Joe and their dad love swimming. The swimming pool is behind the zoo.

The boys like the zoo. There are hippos, tigers and monkeys. There are also elephants. Jim and Joe like the elephants best. They like stroking the elephants' trunks.

Then it is nearly time to go home. Dad and the boys go to the restaurant. Dad has a cup of tea. Joe has an ice cream and Jim has a fruit salad.

13 Now and then

A Listen and look. Talk about the people.

Betty's grandfather is old. His face is wrinkled.

1 
old

2 
young

3 
strong

4 
weak

5 
black hair

6 
grey hair

7 
smooth face

8 
wrinkled face

B Betty's Uncle John was a famous film star. Look at the photos. Act Uncle John.

young / old

legs – strong / weak

thin / fat

hair – black / grey

eyes – good / bad

face – smooth / wrinkled

Now talk about Uncle John's wife.

C Fun Reading

D Act Betty and her grandfather.

1

2

E Read and match.

1 ☐

2 ☐

3 ☐

4 ☐

5 ☐

A 'Hello, Mr West. How are you?'
'Fine, thanks. And you, Cherry?'
'I'm fine, thank you.'

B 'Good morning, Mr West.'
'Good morning, Charlie. You're a good child. I remember you were very short two years ago, but now you're tall.'

C 'Please can I have a balloon?'
'Yes, here you are. One pound, please.'
'Thank you.'

D 'When I was young, I was short but strong. I was good at sports. But now I'm old and weak.'

E 'That's my balloon, not me. I'm down here, Mr West.'
'Oh, I'm sorry. I'm getting old. My eyes were good but they're bad now. I can't see very well.'

14 Camping last summer

A Listen and look at the pictures. What are the children doing?

The children are staying in a tent.
A girl is collecting firewood.

1 
stay in a tent

2 
pack the bags

3 
boil water

4 
cook a meal

5 
wash the dishes

6 
collect firewood

B Look and read. Danny is camping with the Scouts. What did he do yesterday? Act Danny and the Scout leader.

Butterfly Valley Scout Camp

Day 2 Morning

7:00	wash in the river 
7:30	collect firewood 
8:00	boil water for breakfast 
8:30	cook breakfast 
9:00	pack the bags 
9:30	walk to the next camp 

Afternoon

4:30	play games 
6:30	cook dinner 

C Fun Reading

1 Ahmed and Ali were businessmen. They walked a long way in the hot sun.

2 In the evening Ahmed and Ali were very tired. They needed a rest.

3

That night their camel was cold. It opened the tent. It wanted to sleep inside.

4 It pushed Ali out of the tent.

5 The camel went to sleep in the tent.

6 Ahmed pushed the camel and Ali pulled it. But the camel did not move. It stayed in the tent all night.

D Sammy and Julie went to a camp during the summer holidays. Act the children.

1

stay in a camp

2

wash outside

3

climb walls

4

cook our meals

5

play a lot of games

6

walk a long way

E Read and tick (✓) the correct answers.

1 At half past four we collected firewood.

3:30 ☐
4:30 ☐
5:00 ☐

 ☐  ☐  ☐

2 At half past five we boiled water for tea.

4:30 ☐
5:30 ☐
6:30 ☐

 ☐  ☐  ☐

3 At six o'clock we played games.

6:00 ☐
7:00 ☐
7:30 ☐

 ☐  ☐  ☐

4 At half past six we cooked dinner.

6:30 ☐
8:00 ☐
8:30 ☐

 ☐  ☐  ☐

5 At eight o'clock we washed the dishes.

6:30 ☐
7:30 ☐
8:00 ☐

 ☐  ☐  ☐

15 The weather

A Listen and look. What was the weather like last week? What did the children do?

Monday

dry

played outside

Tuesday

hot

swam in the sea

Wednesday

wet and cloudy

stayed inside

Thursday

cold

went shopping

Friday

warm

rode a bicycle

Saturday

windy

climbed a hill

Sunday

sunny

had a picnic

On Monday it was dry.
The children played outside.

B Listen and read. The children are talking about last week. Ask and answer.

1

2

What about you? Ask and answer questions with your friend.

C Fun Reading

1 Yesterday there was a storm. The weather was very bad.

2 The rain was heavy and the wind was strong. Benny and his father only had one umbrella.

3 When they came home, they were very wet.

4 The next day ...

5

6

Choose the best title:

- ☐ The Small Umbrella
- ☐ Getting Wet
- ☐ An Umbrella for Two

D Yesterday there was a storm. Act the teacher and the children.

1

2

What was the weather like yesterday? What did you do?

E Look, read and match.

1 ☐

2 ☐

3 ☐

4 ☐

5 ☐

6 ☐

A Mum had only one umbrella. It was small.

B They walked in the rain. Charlie was not under the umbrella. He got wet.

C Last Saturday morning, the weather was good. Charlie went shopping with his parents.

D Then a taxi went past them and they all got wet.

E In the afternoon, the weather was bad. It was wet and windy.

F The umbrella was too small. So Mum got wet too.

Units 13–15

Revision 5

A Talk about Uncle Ted now and when he was young. Complete the sentences.

1 Uncle Ted … young. Now he … old.
2 His hair … brown. Now it … grey.
3 His face … smooth. Now it … wrinkled.
4 His eyes … good. Now they … bad.

B Read and complete the holiday diary. Use the correct forms of the verbs.

collect	wash	boil
play	get up	cook

Holiday Diary

Yesterday I got up early and I  ______________
my face. Then I  ______________ firewood. After
that I  ______________ some water for tea.
Then I  ______________ breakfast. In the
afternoon I  ______________ games with my friends.

C What was the weather like last week? Ask and answer.

D Talk about what Tim did last week. Use the correct form of the verbs.

Monday

watch a video

Tuesday

go shopping

Wednesday

play outside

Thursday

stay inside

Friday

swim in the sea

Saturday

play computer games

Sunday

have a picnic

E Read: An Adventure Holiday.

Last summer Don and Lilly went on an adventure holiday. They went with the scouts to South Africa. They went on treks in the mountains.

They walked all day. The weather was very hot and the mountains were very beautiful. There were lots of lovely flowers and tall trees. There were also lots of wild animals. The scouts saw deer, monkeys and giraffes.

Every afternoon the scouts made their camp. They put up their tents. Then they washed in a river. After that they collected firewood and boiled water for their dinner. Then they ate their dinner. After dinner they washed up and sat around the campfire and sang songs. They looked up at the stars. They were very tired so they went to bed.

Next day they woke up early and had breakfast. Then they walked to the next camp site.

16 In my kitchen

A Listen and look. What can you see in the kitchen?

1 
some cheese

2 

cat food

3 
some garlic

4 
an onion

5 
a pineapple

6 
a rubbish bin

B Listen and read. The children are asking about the things in their kitchens. Ask and answer.

1

2

Play the games.

C Fun Reading

1

2

3

4

5

6

D **Charlie is looking at his mother's shopping. Act Charlie and his mother.**

1

2

3

E Read and tick (✓) or cross (✗).

This is Mrs Johnson's kitchen. It's big. You can see a rubbish bin and some dishes. There's a table in the kitchen too. On it, there's some cheese, some garlic, some vegetables, pineapples and some meat balls. The cheese smells strong, but the pineapples smell nice. There's some cat food too. Can you see the bananas? They smell nice, don't they?

1 It is Mrs Brown's kitchen. ☐

2 The kitchen is big. ☐

3 Mike thinks the cheese smells strong. ☐

4 Mike doesn't like the smell of pineapples. ☐

5 Mike likes the smell of bananas. ☐

17 Sounds we hear

A Listen and look. What is happening?

A dog is barking.
People are shouting.

1 
barking

2 
laughing

3 
crying

4 
talking

5 
shouting

6 
snoring

7 
banging

8 
singing

B Listen and read. Cherry is in the park with her grandmother.

Now you are Cherry's grandmother. What else can you hear?

C Fun Reading

1 Last night Eric Taylor could not sleep.

2 Suddenly Eric heard a noise. He thought there was a robber outside in the corridor.

3

Eric picked up a vase standing on the bedside table.

4

The door opened. Eric raised the vase to smash it on the robber's head.

5 Suddenly the light went on. It was his wife.

Act the story.

D Susan and Cherry cannot sleep. Ask and answer.

Say Susan's poem.

When I lie in bed at night,
I can hear my father,
I can hear him laughing, laughing,
When I lie in bed at night.

Now can you say Cherry's poem?

E Look and tick (✓) or cross (✗).

1

2

3

4

5

6

7

8

9

10

11

12

1 Some water is falling. ☐

2 Two dogs are barking. ☐

3 A man is snoring. ☐

4 A workman is banging. ☐

5 Some children are pushing a camel. ☐

6 A young woman is packing a bag. ☐

7 Two girls are collecting firewood. ☐

8 An old woman is boiling water. ☐

9 A woman is shouting. ☐

10 A cat is climbing the tree. ☐

11 Two women are laughing. ☐

12 A baby is crying. ☐

18 A good brother

A Read and listen to the story.

1

Jerry was thirteen and Winnie was six. Jerry loved his little sister.

2

Winnie did not want to stay at home.

3

Jerry did not like getting wet but he wanted to make his sister happy.

4

Jerry took off his shoes. Then he rolled up his trousers and walked into the river.

5

6

Jerry took off his T-shirt and ran after the butterfly. He followed it round and round.

7

Jerry did not see a big stone on the ground. He tripped over it and hit his head.

8

Jerry was tired and dirty. There was a big hole in his T-shirt. He went to his room and fell asleep on the bed.

9 That night Winnie could not sleep. She thought about her brother. She was sad.

10

Winnie went into the kitchen. She took a cake out of the fridge.

11 Winnie went into her brother's room and gave him the cake.

12

Mrs Williams smiled as she watched the children.

B Put the sentences in the right order. Write the numbers in the boxes.

☐ a) Winnie was sorry for Jerry. She gave him a cake.

☐ b) Jerry tried to catch it but he could not.

☐ c) Jerry was tired. He fell asleep and did not have any dinner.

☐ d) Winnie wanted a crab. Jerry caught it for her.

☐ e) One day Jerry and Winnie went out to play.

☐ f) Then Winnie wanted a butterfly.

C Complete the sentences. Use the correct form of these words.

take like catch want sleep look after see	did not

Picture 1: Jerry looked after his sister.

Picture 2: Winnie ______________ to stay at home.

Picture 3: Jerry ______________ getting wet.

Picture 4: Jerry ______________ the crab.

Picture 7: Jerry ______________ a big stone on the ground.

Picture 9: Winnie could ______________ that night.

Picture 10: Winnie ______________ a cake out of the fridge.

D Winnie wrote a letter to her friend Rose. Finish the letter for her.

Dear Rose,

Yesterday I went out to play with my brother. We (1) ______ to the river. At the river I saw a crab. My brother (2)  ______ it for me. Then I (3) ______ a butterfly. My brother tried to catch it but he could not. He (4) ______ over a big stone and (5)  ______ his head.

My brother was very tired when we got home. He (6) ______ asleep. He did not have any dinner. He was very hungry. Later in the night I (7)  ______ him a cake. I said sorry too. I love my brother and he loves me.

Yours,
Winnie

E Read and tick the correct responses.

1

Mum, this afternoon I washed the dishes, I watered the plants and I fed the dog.

- [ ] Sorry, Jerry.
- [ ] Thank you, Jerry.

2

I did my homework too, Mum.

- [ ] Good boy!
- [ ] Naughty boy!

3

Sit down, Mum. Do you want a drink?

- [ ] Goodbye.
- [ ] Yes, please.

4

I painted a picture for you, Mum.

- [ ] Oh dear!
- [ ] It's beautiful.

5

But Winnie, look at your dress. It's so dirty.

- [ ] Sorry, Mum.
- [ ] That's all right.

Revision 6

A What can you see in the picture? Ask and tick.

B Look, read and match.

1 Can you hear a man?
2 Can you hear a bird?
3 Can you hear some children?
4 Can you hear a woman?

Can you hear them?
Can you hear him?
Can you hear her?
Can you hear it?

C What did Simon do yesterday? Look and say.

ride his bike	play basketball	go to school
swim in the sea	have lunch	watch TV

In the morning

In the afternoon

D Beeno went on holiday. What did he pack? Listen and tick.

umbrella  ☐

raincoat  ☐

book  ☐

boots 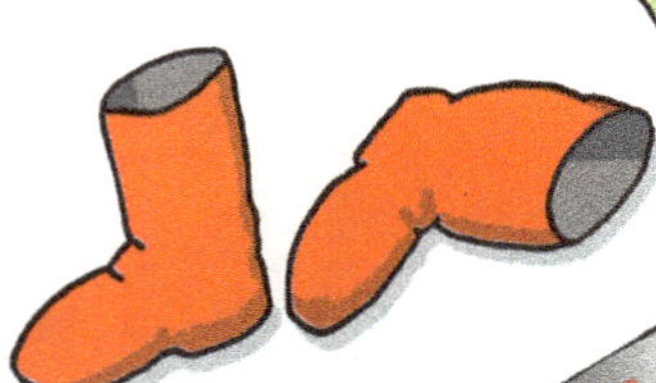 ☐

biscuits 

☐

toy rabbit  ☐

E Read: Grandpa's Birthday.

Yesterday it was Grandpa's birthday so Tessa and Susie's mother cooked a special dinner for Grandpa and Grandma. The girls helped their mother. Tessa prepared some vegetables and Susie helped Mother cook some chicken. The food smelled delicious.

Then Tessa put some fruit in a bowl. First she put some oranges in the bowl. Then she put in some strawberries. After that she put some grapes on top of the fruit in the bowl.

Susie laid the table for dinner. She put the bowl of fruit on the table. Next to the fruit bowl she put a vase of flowers and Grandpa's birthday cake. Everything was ready.

At eight o'clock the girls heard the door open. Dad came in with Grandpa and Grandma. Then Uncle Jack, Uncle Jim and Aunt Kathy came. The whole family had a lovely meal.

After dinner, everyone sang Happy Birthday Dear Grandpa and gave him a birthday card and a present. Then it was time for the birthday cake. It was delicious. Grandpa told lots of stories and jokes. Everyone had a lovely time and the girls stayed up late.

Pearson Education Limited
Edinburgh Gate, Harlow
Essex CM20 2JE
United Kingdom
and Associated Companies throughout the World.

www.longman.com

© Pearson Education Limited 2005

Adaptation copyright © 2004 by Pearson Education Limited
Original edition copyright © Pearson Education Asia Limited 2000
All Rights Reserved.
Published by arrangement with the original publisher,
Pearson Education Asia Limited, a Pearson Education company.

First Published in 2005
ISBN 140 58 0265 0

ARP impression 98

Set in Longman English 14pt
Printed in Great Britain by Ashford Colour Press Ltd
Prepared for the Publishers by
HDA, Brighton BN2 1GZ England

Illustration
Seth Cook, Trevor Cook,
Sally Henry, David Heywood,
Arthur Phillips, Katy Sleight

Photography
We are grateful to the following for permission to reproduce copyright photographs:
Alan Levenson / Powerstock for page 18 (*top left*) and page 90 (*middle left*);
Steve Kronqard / Getty Images for page 18 (*bottom left*);
Corbis for page 36 (*top*);
Sally Henry / HDA for page 36 (*middle right*) and page 108 (*bottom left*);
Judith Miller / Dorling Kindersley for page 36 (*bottom middle*);
Paul Bricknell / Dorling Kindersley for page 36 (*bottom right*);
Dave Winter / Photo & Co. / Corbis for page 54 (*top right*);
Ian Hodgson / Reuters / Corbis for page 54 (*bottom left*);
Robin Smith / Getty Images for page 72 (*top left*);
SW Productions /Getty Images for page 72 (*middle left*);
Patrik Giardino / Corbis for page 72 (*middle right*);
Gerald French / Corbis for page 72 (*bottom left*);
Jennie Woodcock / Bubbles for page 90 (*top right*);
Torleif Svensson / Corbis for page 90 (*middle left*);
Mary Ann McDonald / Corbis for page 90 (*bottom right*);
Creatas for page 108 (*top*).